D... ...RUG
BEGINNERS

CAR ●
DRIVING ●
FOR ●
BEGINNERS

Published in collaboration with the Royal Automobile Club

Adam and Charles Black

Text and photographs copyright © EP Publishing Limited
1960, 1983; © A & C Black (Publishers) Limited 1984

British Library Cataloguing in Publication Data

Royal Automobile Club
  Car driving for beginners.
  1. Automobile driving
  I. Title
  629.28'32   TL152.5

ISBN 0-7136-2588-0

First edition 1960
Fourth edition 1983
Fifth edition, completely revised, 1984
Published by A & C Black (Publishers) Limited
35 Bedford Row, London, WC1R 4JH

Printed and bound in Great Britain
by Hollen Street Press Ltd, Slough, Berkshire

Design and illustrations: Brian L. Ainsworth

Photographs: Handford Photography/Robert Pyke

Contents

How to use this book

A book cannot teach you to drive; it can only be a supplement to your instruction and your driving practice. These pages, however, if studied carefully before and after your driving lessons, will not only help to speed you through your test, but will show you how to become an expert and safe driver.

The book is divided into three parts. The first deals with how a car works. It is assumed that the reader knows nothing about this subject, and as some slight knowledge is helpful, the first few pages deal with the clutch and gears in a very simple, non-technical way.

The second part of the book explains 'road sense' and shows you how to negotiate the main hazards which will be met on the road.

The third part deals with taking the driving test and some typical questions on the Highway Code are included. The Highway Code is, of course, essential reading. It explains clearly and authoritatively the etiquette of the road and you cannot expect to pass your test unless you have studied it carefully.

Part 1: How the car works

The controls

The main controls, which you must know before you can start to drive, are the accelerator, clutch, gear lever, foot brake and hand brake. There are minor controls for ignition and starter, choke (if the choke is not automatic), indicators, horn, lights, windscreen wash/wipers and heater.

Accelerator pedal

The accelerator pedal is operated by the right foot. When pressed, it increases the speed of the engine and thus gives more power. Likewise, when the pedal is released the engine speed decreases and the engine loses some of its power.

Clutch pedal

The clutch pedal is operated by the left foot. When pressed, this pedal disconnects the engine from the gear box, so that the gear lever can be moved into different positions. When released (gently) it re-connects the engine to the gear box.

Gear lever

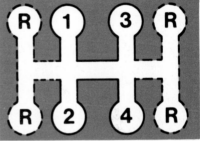

The number of forward gears, with the gear lever position to select them or reverse gear, may vary according to model of car but their use is always the same. In the explanations that follow it is presumed that the gear lever is pivoted on the floor to the left of the driver, or on the steering column below the steering wheel (this is now unusual).

Diagram 1 The usual position of the gears. Reverse may be in any one of the four positions shown

   When the engine is 'running' the gear lever can be moved into different positions as in the above example only when the clutch pedal is pressed down.

(Foot) brake pedal

Also operated by the right foot, this pedal is used for slowing down or stopping the car.

Hand brake

The hand brake is found between the front seats, or underneath the dashboard or on the right of the driver's seat, with a ratchet to hold it in the 'on' position. The hand brake should be used to hold the car when parked, when stationary in traffic or when on a hill. As it works on two wheels only (usually the rear wheels) and could cause a skid on the move it should not be used to stop the car when moving except in an emergency as when other brakes fail.

Choke

The choke, although, not a major control, is included here because many learner drivers have difficulty with it at first. The choke is a valve which controls the inflow of air to the engine; when in use it increases the proportion of petrol in the fuel mixture. Some cars have an automatic choke; if it is manual, there is a choke button which is out for full choke and in for no choke. Full choke should be used when starting the car when the engine is cold; the choke is then progressively reduced as the engine warms up. Incorrect positioning of the choke control will cause the engine to labour or stall. Choke should not be used when the engine has warmed up to its normal running temperature.

Photo 3 The controls

The pedals

Accelerator

This pedal is operated by the right foot and it controls the speed of the engine; when the car is moving it also controls the speed of the car.

When the engine is started (with your foot off the accelerator), you will find that the engine will run slowly — it is said to 'idle' or 'tick over'. When the accelerator is pressed, the engine speeds up; when it is released the engine slows down. Although, when the car is moving, taking your foot off the accelerator pedal slows down the car to some extent, it is not sufficient to stop it completely and the foot brake has to be used.

Brake (foot)

The brake and accelerator pedals are never used at the same time, so the right foot is used to control both pedals. It is important to practise until the right foot can be moved freely and with certainty from one pedal to the other.

The brake pedal should be pressed gently at first and pressure gradually increased to bring the car to a stop more quickly. If it is pressed too quickly the car will stop with a violent jolt.

Clutch

This pedal is always operated by the left foot. When the pedal is pressed, the plates of the clutch are separated and the engine is disconnected from the gear-box. When the pedal is released, the clutch plates come together and the engine is again connected to the gear-box (see pages 10-12).

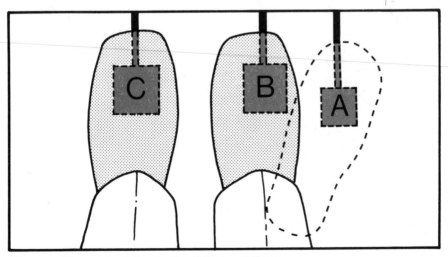

Diagram 2 The pedals A: Accelerator B: Brake C: Clutch

How the clutch works

Careful control of the clutch pedal is essential at all times and is one of the most important factors in good driving. The clutch enables the drive to the gear-box to be connected and disconnected so that the car can move off smoothly without jerking and the gears can be changed easily and quietly.

In Diag. 3 full depression of the clutch pedal is holding the driven plate B away from the flywheel A, so no engine drive is reaching the gear-box.

Diag. 4 shows the 'biting' or 'take-up' point (this varies with different cars and has to be found by trial and error): the clutch plates (A and B) are just together but are slipping.

The next slight decrease of pressure on the pedal will give a smooth take-up between the engine and the gear-box. When the pedal is fully released (Diag. 5), plate B is pressed firmly against plate A by springs, giving a solid connection between engine and gear-box. If the clutch pedal is released suddenly, the engine will stop or 'stall'.

Only in the position shown in Diag. 4 does the clutch pedal position create any noticeable change — starting to connect or disconnect engine drive to the gear-box.

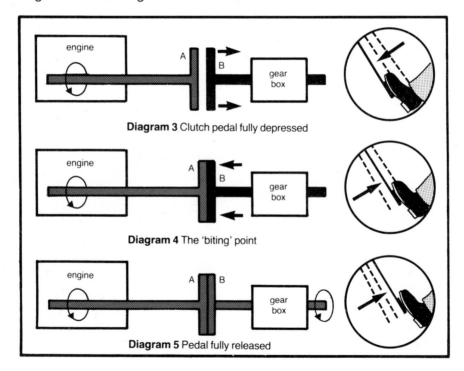

Diagram 3 Clutch pedal fully depressed

Diagram 4 The 'biting' point

Diagram 5 Pedal fully released

10

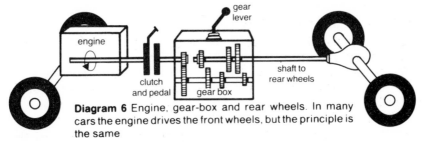

Diagram 6 Engine, gear-box and rear wheels. In many cars the engine drives the front wheels, but the principle is the same

Action of clutch and gears

Diags. 7 – 13 show what happens in the gear-box when you move the clutch pedal and gear lever.

Diag. 7 *Engine running. Gear lever in neutral. Clutch pedal released.* The gear-wheels on the shaft to the rear wheels do not mesh with any of the others, so do not turn. To make the car move it is necessary to connect two of the gear-wheels.

Diag. 8 *Clutch pedal depressed.* This disconnects the engine from the gear-box: all the gear-wheels are stationary, so can be moved to engage one another as required.

Diag. 9 *Clutch pedal still depressed. Gear lever moved into first gear position (low).* Large gear on shaft to rear wheels connected to small gear.

Diag. 10 *Clutch released.* The clutch pedal should be released gently as explained on page 10 to close the plates of the clutch and so re-connect the engine to the gear-box and thus to the rear wheels. Notice that the engine turns quickly compared with shaft to rear wheels.

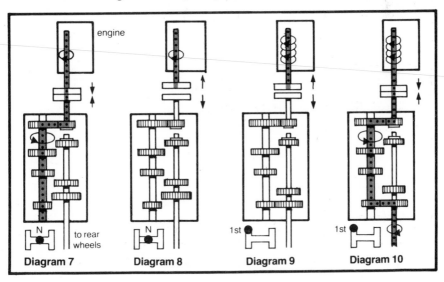

Diagram 7 Diagram 8 Diagram 9 Diagram 10

11

Diag. 11 *Gear lever moved into second gear position.* Shaft to rear wheels increased in speed relative to engine speed.

Diag. 12 *Gear lever moved into third gear position.* Shaft to rear wheels increased still more in speed relative to engine speed.

Diag. 13 *Gear lever moved into fourth gear position.* Shaft to rear wheels driven direct from engine shaft. A fifth gear, if fitted, is a higher gear or overdrive.

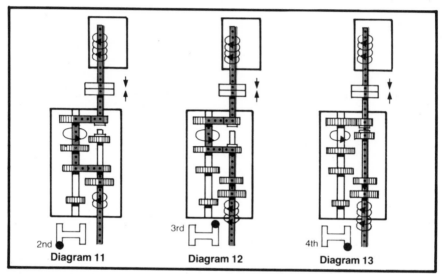

| Diagram 11 | Diagram 12 | Diagram 13 |

Remember that, when the car is stopping, the rear wheels, through the gears, are connected to the engine. If the rear wheels stop then the engine will also stop unless the clutch pedal is pressed down to separate the driven clutch plate from the flywheel and so disconnect the engine.

When the engine 'labours' it is turning too slowly to exert the necessary power.

The car is usually started off by using the lowest, slowest and most powerful forward gear, that is first gear. The power is needed, when starting off, to overcome the inertia or dead weight of the car. Once the car is moving, its momentum and impetus are assisting the engine and it is then possible to 'change up' to the next gear (second) which is a faster gear but not so powerful as first — so more speed is obtained with less power. As the speed increases, so higher gears can be engaged until top or high gear is reached. Top gear is the fastest yet the least powerful of the gears.

Most manual gear-change cars have four or five forward gears. The speed for changing gear varies considerably with the car and road conditions but Diag. 14 shows the approximate speeds at which the gears might be changed in economical driving to the next highest for a 5-speed gear-box. Where there is a fifth gear, this provides lower engine speed for economical cruising.

The position of the gear lever for reverse gear varies according to the type and make of the car and possible positions are as shown.

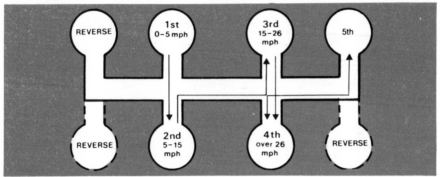

Diagram 14 5-speed gear-box: approximate speeds for changing up on level road

Automatic transmission

With automatic transmission there is no clutch pedal to be used in co-ordination with the accelerator and hand brake. Selector settings may differ between different makes, and manufacturer's instructions for their use must be closely followed.

Generally there are three forward gears which the transmission itself selects according to engine load, but others have two gears or four.

For most forward driving the selector lever should remain in Drive, remaining there with the hand brake on for stops of short duration, as at a red traffic light. For longer stops with the engine running the selector should be placed in Neutral and in Park when parked or with the engine switched off; in both cases the hand brake should be applied.

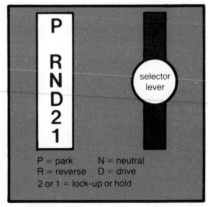

Diagram 15 A typical automatic gear control

Where the facility to Lock up or Hold certain gears is provided, makers' instructions for correct use should be fully understood, although in the driving test a demonstration of knowledge of such use may only be called for if applicable conditions are encountered. The

13

commonest example of such conditions is when driving up or down steep gradients; if not held in second (or first) gear the car may sometimes change into top gear undesirably, causing the engine to lose revolutions going uphill, or requiring undue use of the brakes going downhill.

Many automatic cars have a so-called 'kick-down' switch: when the accelerator is quickly and completely depressed, the transmission automatically changes down a gear, providing extra acceleration when needed for overtaking or to avoid danger.

When driving an automatic car, the right foot only should be used for the accelerator or brake, even though there is no clutch pedal for the left foot to operate. It may, however, be convenient and safe to use the left foot on the brake when manoeuvring slowly with a minimum of acceleration.

In Britain passing a test on a car with manual gear change carries an entitlement also to drive cars with automatic transmission; but passing the test on an automatic car does not carry entitlement to drive cars with manual gear change.

Diagram 16 Transverse solid white line (stop line).
Where traffic must stop when required by police or light signals

Diagram 17 Transverse solid white line.
Where traffic must stop, at a stop sign.

Diagram 18 Transverse double broken white lines.
Where traffic must give way to traffic on major road, sometimes preceded by a 'Give Way' sign

Solid or broken white lines are used in various places to indicate the edge of the carriageway at a road junction or lay-by, etc.

Yellow broken lines, or yellow solid or yellow double solid lines running alongside the kerb edge indicate that waiting and parking are restricted as indicated by signs on nearby posts

Part 2: On the road
Traffic signs
Some traffic signs are shown in the Highway Code and for your test you will need to know and be able to describe all those in current use. Some are shown here and where necessary are explained below.

1. Keep left
2. No entry
3. All vehicles prohibited
4. All motor vehicles prohibited
5. Turn left ahead
6. No stopping ('Clearway')
7. No waiting
8. No overtaking
12. Uneven road
13. Slippery road
14. Crossroads
15. Danger
16. Distance to stop line ahead
17. No through road
19. Priority over vehicles from opposite direction
21. Appropriate traffic lanes at junction ahead

For full description see the HMSO booklet *Know Your Traffic Signs.*

Diagram 19

A. Signs which INSTRUCT have a circle . . . though a few have a triangle or an octagon as below.

Red circle PROHIBITS or RESTRICTS

Blue circle is MANDATORY (tells you what to do)

B. Signs which WARN and INFORM have a red triangle. Here are a few:

C. Signs which give OTHER INFORMATION are usually on a rectangle. Here are a few:

15

Traffic lights

When STATIONARY
Wait behind STOP line on carriageway

Prepare to move; engage low gear.
Place hand on hand brake. Do not move off on the red–amber but get ready to start promptly on green, if safe to do so

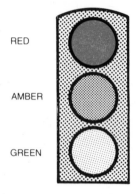

RED

AMBER

GREEN

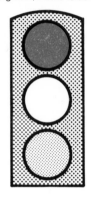

When APPROACHING
Slow down gradually and stop before the line

Slow down and do not pass the stop line until light changes to green

When STATIONARY
You may go on if the way is clear.
Take special care if turning left or right, and give way to any pedestrians who are crossing

Do not move: remain behind STOP line

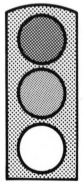

Diagram 20

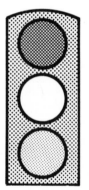

When APPROACHING
Be ready to stop, but go on if the way is clear. Do not race in an attempt to cross before the green changes

Means STOP! Slow down and stop unless you have crossed the stop line or are so close to it that to pull up might cause an accident

Pelican crossings (PEdestrian LIght CONtrolled) These have the normal colour sequence except that instead of red/amber there is a flashing amber, which indicates that drivers must give way to pedestrians on the crossing but may proceed if the crossing is clear.

You and the law
The law states that you must ...
- not drive while under the influence of *drink* or *drugs*
- have a current *driving licence* (signed in ink) valid for the vehicle you are driving
- be *insured* to cover liability in respect of any third-party risk
- wear your seatbelt when driving (except when reversing)
- be in a position where you can control the car properly and see the road ahead clearly
- always switch off the engine and set the hand brake securely before leaving the car
- not park your car so that it causes an unnecessary obstruction
- park on the left at night except in one-way streets; side and tail lights must be lit unless there is a 30 mph (or less) limit, the car is close to and parallel with the kerb and not within 15 yards of a junction
- use headlamps (or sidelights with paired fog/spotlights) in poor daytime visibility
- by night use headlamps on all roads where there is no street lighting and dipped headlamps in built-up areas unless the street lighting is so good that they are not needed

Diagram 21 Be in a position where you can see the road ahead clearly.

The law states your car must have . . .

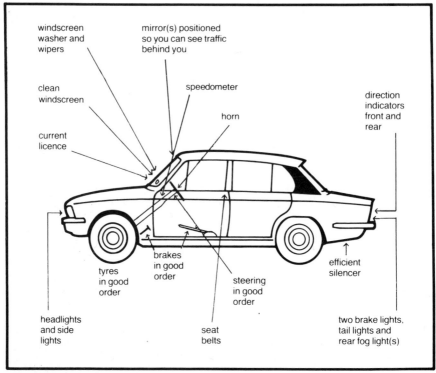

Diagram 22

- When moving on an unlit road in the dark, or in bad visibility by day, you must have switched on at least one pair of headlights matched in position, area, shape and colour (white or yellow), switching on and off at the same time and emitting either main or dipped beams together. A single fog lamp may only be used with two headlamps.
- Lights must be in working order by day as well as night.
- Seat belts must be fitted to front seats of all cars registered on or after 1 January, 1965.
- Tyres must be suitable for the vehicle, properly inflated, have a depth of tread of at least 1 mm over three-quarters of the whole surface with a visible tread pattern on the remaining surface, and be free from cuts and other defects. You may not put radials on the front only or on the same axle as cross-ply.
- Your car must have a current MoT test certificate if more than three years old.

- The load on your vehicle must not be excessive nor so badly packed as to be dangerous.
- Motor Vehicle Regulations are published in H.M.S.O. pamphlets from time to time and you are expected to know these.
- The correct fitting of one or two rear fog lights of approved design is a legal requirement for cars manufactured on or after 1 October, 1979 and first used on or after 1 April, 1980.
- Your car must be in good condition, not noisy and not emitting fumes and smoke.
- Readable number plates (rear illuminated at night). (These must be reflective if the car was first registered on or after 1 January, 1973.)
- *Important:* Read 'The Law's demands' in the Highway Code.

Driving position

The correct driving position (Photo 4) is very important: you must be high enough to be able to see the road ahead without having to peer over the top of the steering wheel and also to get your arm out of the window for signalling. This means that a short person may need a cushion to sit on.

If necessary the seat should be adjusted forward, or backward, or a cushion placed behind you so that you can reach the pedals without having to stretch and without being too cramped. You should be able to press the clutch pedal right down with the left foot and still have the left knee slightly bent. If this can be done, then the foot brake and accelerator can also be reached with the right foot.

You must have free individual leg movement and this means sitting with your knees slightly apart.

Adjust the mirror so that you can see the road behind clearly.

Photo 4 The correct position: clear view of road ahead and legs not cramped or stretched

Steering

The position of your hands on the steering wheel is very important if you are to get maximum power and freedom of movement. The best position is at or between 'ten to two' or 'a quarter to three'.

Keep a firm but relaxed grip and never rest your elbow on the window frame. Beginners often 'oversteer', that is they grip the wheel too hard and turn the wheel too far for the change of direction required, thus making the car zig-zag. Remember that on a flat road the car will tend to run on a straight course and very little movement of the steering wheel is necessary when you want to change direction slightly.

Practise driving along a straight road to get the 'feel' of the steering, keeping the car about four feet from the kerb.

Always keep both hands on the wheel if possible, but it is necessary to be able to steer competently with one hand whilst changing gear or signalling. Never cross your hands on the wheel; this is dangerous and may lead to loss of control; and never let the wheel spin free. When the wheel is fully turned in either direction it is said to be 'on full lock'.

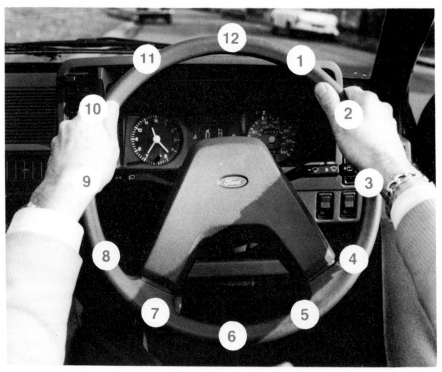

Photo 5 Hold the wheel at the 'ten to two' position

Turning left and right

To turn the wheel at a corner, the hands are used alternately in a 'push–pull' action. 'Feed' the steering wheel through your hands and never cross them over.

Diagram 23 Turning left
Pull down on the wheel with your left hand, allowing the wheel to travel through your right hand, then push up with your right hand, and so on

Diagram 24 Turning right
Pull down with your right hand, allowing the wheel to travel through your left hand, then push up with your left hand

Wheel tracks

When the car is on a curved course, the rear wheels always run inside the track of the front wheels: that may cause them to 'cut the corner' as shown in Photo 6 and Diag. 25.

Photo 6 Wrong: Front wheels are clear of kerb but rear wheels have mounted pavement

Diagram 25

Always make sure you have plenty of room on the inside of the curve, remembering that when the front wheels are fully turned, the rear end of the car may need a further two feet or more to clear any obstruction.

Do not swing out before turning.

Moving off

Preliminary checks on entering the car are that (a) all doors are properly closed and fastened, (b) the driving seat is adjusted, (c) mirrors are correctly adjusted and clean, (d) you and your passengers have fastened your seat belts, and (e) there is enough petrol. Drill for starting the engine is then to check that (a) the hand brake is on, by pulling it further, (b) the gear lever is in neutral, (c) the choke is correctly adjusted. Then turn the key in the ignition switch and start the engine.

Now, assuming the car is on level ground you must:
1. Press the clutch pedal and hold it down.
2. Move the gear lever into first gear.
3. Press the accelerator pedal slightly to speed up the engine (but do not let it roar) and hold the accelerator pedal steady in this position.
4. Gently release pressure on the clutch pedal until it reaches the critical, or 'biting' point. This is the moment at which the clutch takes up the power and you will soon learn to recognise it by feel and by the change in the engine sound.
5. Look in the mirror and look over your right shoulder to make sure it is safe to pull out from the kerb.

6. If there is any other road user who would be helped by the information, give a clear signal to indicate that you are about to pull out. This can either be made by hand (see Diag. 26) or mechanically as long as the signal is fully visible.
7. When sure it is safe to move, gently release the clutch pedal, at the same time releasing the hand brake; the car will move slowly forward. The accelerator pedal now controls the speed of the car.
8. Pull away from the kerb — taking care to ensure that it is safe to move off (Photo 7).

The sequence of actions involved in moving off should be practised many times until the car can be moved smoothly without jerking and without stalling the engine. The most important contribution to a smooth start is your use of the clutch pedal's 'biting' point. Remember that the changing sound of the engine will always help you to recognise this.

Photo 7 Make sure it is safe before pulling away from the kerb

Hill start

Starting on an uphill gradient is similar, but you must prevent the car rolling backwards downhill when the hand brake is released. Here is the correct sequence:
1. Press the clutch pedal and hold it down.
2. Engage first gear.
3. Press the accelerator pedal a little more than you would if starting on the flat and hold it in that position.
4. Release clutch pedal gently until it gets to the biting point.
5. Hold the clutch still at this point, then
6. make sure it is safe to move off and signal as necessary, as before and
7. do the following three movements together: accelerate a little more (the amount will depend on the steepness of the hill), release hand brake slowly and release clutch pedal slowly.

If the car rolls backwards the hand brake has been released before the clutch has taken up the power.

If the engine stalls, either the clutch has been released too rapidly, or the accelerator has not been pressed sufficiently.

Signals

Always signal in good time, having checked in front and behind if there are any pedestrians and drivers who will need to know your intentions. Normally signal by braking lights or direction indicators but at pedestrian crossings when slowing or stopping signal by arm.

I intend to move out to the right or turn right

I intend to move in to the left or turn left (*indicator*: or stop on the left)

I intend to slow down or stop

Diagram 26 Arm signals

Changing gear

When changing gear, place the left hand on top of the lever, with the palm away from you when engaging 1st or 2nd gear, and with the palm towards you when changing into 3rd, 4th or 5th gear.

Practise placing your hand on the gear lever in its different positions without looking down. Changing gear without taking your eyes off the road is another vital point in good, safe driving.

Changing 'Up'

As explained on pages 11–12 the car is usually started in first gear because it is the most powerful. As soon as the car's speed reaches about 5 to 7 mph you must change up to second gear (see Diag. 27). Though changing up has been divided here into three separate stages, you should practise until changing gear becomes a smooth rhythmic movement.

Use the same method to change up from second to third, from third to fourth gear (in a car with four forward gears) and from fourth to fifth (in a car with five forward gears).

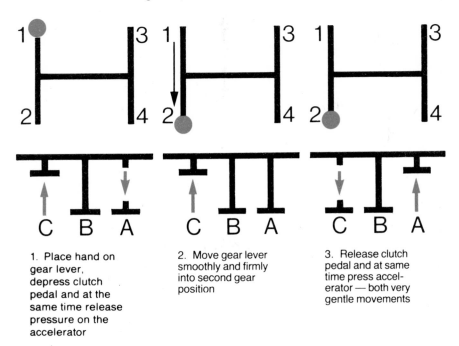

1. Place hand on gear lever, depress clutch pedal and at the same time release pressure on the accelerator

2. Move gear lever smoothly and firmly into second gear position

3. Release clutch pedal and at same time press accelerator — both very gentle movements

Diagram 27

25

Changing 'Down'

You may need to change down to a lower gear to keep going more slowly, to be able to pull away or accelerate, or on hills (see page 28), and Diag. 28 shows the sequence, with a change from 4th to 3rd. You may change down direct to the gear needed, without first using an intermediate gear, provided the car is at the correct corresponding speed and engine speed is suitably adjusted as in Diag. 28 (1). The amount of extra engine speed needed, if any, will be learned by experience. It depends on the new gear chosen, the car's speed and the rate at which the car slows down when changing gear on a hill.

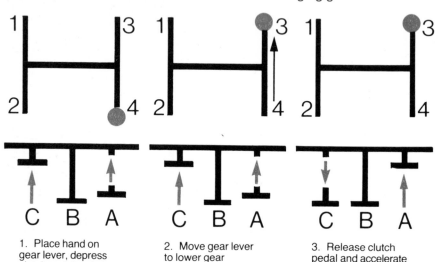

1. Place hand on gear lever, depress clutch pedal and at the same time keep accelerator slightly depressed

2. Move gear lever to lower gear position

3. Release clutch pedal and accelerate or decelerate as required

Diagram 28

Driving drill

Remember: Mirror — Signal — Manoeuvre (MSM)

Look in the mirror to see what traffic is behind you.

Manoeuvre involves 'PSL': taking up correct Position, adjusting Speed and Look where necessary to see if the manoeuvre is safe.

Decide in good time what course to follow to the correct position, the speed adjustment needed, and what signal is necessary.

Look in the mirror again to make sure it is safe, give the correct signal and then commence the manoeuvre.

When slowing down for a corner or other hazard, release the accelerator early and then brake if further slowing is needed. If braking is necessary, apply the foot brake early and steadily (not suddenly) until your speed is slow and safe enough for the approaching hazard. Then change into the appropriate gear (see Diag. 28). If slowing down to alter course or position, brake lights, if braking, with an indicator signal of the intended manoeuvre, given in good time, are sufficient indication. But when it is not obvious that you are slowing, and others should know, give the slowdown arm signal.

Photo 8 Parts of the car can hide pedestrians — make *sure* the road is clear. Here a pedestrian is only just visible in the rear side window

When changing direction your view to the side may be obstructed by parts of the car — Photo 8 — so make sure the road is clear by moving your head until you can see clearly.

Stopping

Make sure it is safe to stop by looking in the mirror, then if necessary give the left indicator signal, remove your foot from the accelerator and press the brake pedal steadily (don't jab it). When the car has almost stopped, press the clutch pedal as well and hold it down. The clutch must be pressed and held before the car has stopped, otherwise the engine will stall. When stationary, apply the hand brake and release pressure on the foot brake. Then move the gear lever into neutral and take your foot off the clutch pedal.

In an emergency stop, mirror and signals are secondary to control. Keep both hands on the steering wheel, try not to lock the wheels, and de-clutch as above.

Uphill and downhill

When the car is climbing a hill more power and engine speed are needed to push it up the gradient. Increased accelerator pressure is required to obtain these, and if the extra power is still insufficient it will be necessary to change to a lower gear. The 'change down' is made as soon as the engine does not respond freely to the accelerator.

'Changing down' on a rising gradient must be done with as little loss of time as possible because the car is losing speed rapidly. The movements are shown in Diag. 28.

If the car does not respond in the new gear because it is insufficiently low or the gradient is increasing then you should change to the next lower gear using the same sequence (see Diag. 29).

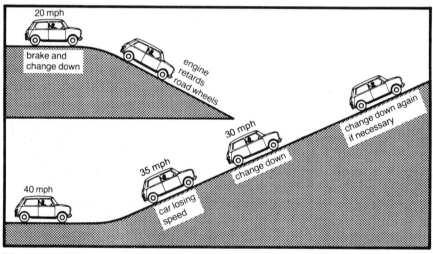

Diagram 29 Ascending and descending a steep hill

Ascending a very steep hill, if the gear change is made too slowly, the car may stop and eventually start to run backwards. The hand brake must then be used immediately and the car re-started as for a hill start (see page 23).

When descending a hill, lower gears may be used to help control the speed. Select a suitable gear before commencing the descent. If much braking is still required to keep the car from gaining speed downhill, you should engage a still lower gear to assist the brake, as lower gears are slower gears. The use of clutch and gear lever is the same as for an uphill change, but when descending the right foot is used on the foot brake instead of the accelerator, to prevent the car gaining speed as the gear lever is moved. In an automatic car, use the lock-up or hold to maintain a low gear.

How to turn left

Remember 'MSM'. When still some distance from the turning, look in the mirror and give the left indicator signal, timed so that it clearly shows in advance which turning you are taking. Be careful to see and allow safe passage for cyclists or motorcyclists coming up on your left. For the second 'M' of 'MSM' — Manoeuvre — consider 'PSL': Position, Speed, Look. The car should be positioned approximately three to four feet from the left-hand kerb and slowed by releasing the accelerator pedal, if necessary using the foot brake. Then, with the left indicator still going, change to a suitable low gear, usually second, remembering never to pull out to the right.

Arrive at the corner below 10 mph. If there is an approach from the right, look right, then left and right again and be prepared to stop. Keep looking. When the car is round the corner straighten the steering wheel but do not accelerate until the car is on a straight course again.

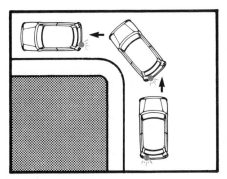

Diagram 30 Correct way to turn left

Correct way to turn left:
Photo 9 Car not swinging out to the right

Photo 10 Rear wheel clear of kerb on corner

Photo 11 Keep looking, and ensure that the road is clear

Photo 12 Car too close to kerb at start of turn results in . . .

Photo 13 Easing out to the right to clear the kerb which may endanger following traffic

Photo 14 Rear wheels running over the pavement corner. This endangers pedestrians and damages the tyres

Photo 15 Swinging out too far into adjoining road, thus endangering facing traffic

How to turn right

Remember: Mirror, Signal, Manoeuvre (Position, Speed, Look). Well before you reach the turning, look in the mirror and if safe, make the 'moving right' indicator signal and steer the car gradually over to the middle of the road, keeping just to the left of the centre. Keep the right indicator on, slow down, change into a lower gear, approach cautiously, look in mirror again and observe traffic right, left and on-coming. If safe to do so turn right, steering carefully round the centre of the road junction (Diag. 31).

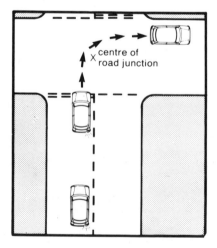

centre of road junction

Diagram 31 Correct way to turn right

If not safe, STOP and wait, getting into first gear and holding hand brake on. Keep looking. Never cut across oncoming traffic. If an approaching car intends to turn to its right, it is safer if possible to pass right-hand to right-hand, i.e. behind the other vehicle, but there may be occasions when the road markings indicate otherwise or the type of crossing makes this impracticable, in which case extra care is needed to observe vehicles hidden behind the approaching car.

When turning give precedence to pedestrians crossing the side road.

Photo 16 **Photo 17**
Correct. Car approaching junction just to the left of the centre of the road (photo 16) and turning round the centre of the junction (photo 17)

Photo 18 Not signalling in good time may delay traffic which could have passed on left

Photo 19 Pulling over without using the mirror or signalling endangers following traffic

Photo 20 Keeping to the left on wide roads and signalling a turn to the right disorganises following traffic

Photo 21 Cutting the corner too soon means that you will cross the line of oncoming traffic

Reversing

Much care and practice are needed to develop the necessary judgement for reversing confidently round a corner or into an opening. Before reversing, always make sure that it is safe to do so. If necessary get out of the car and look behind it. Do not reverse into a main road. Do not reverse such a distance as to cause inconvenience to other road users.

1. Always check all round for other traffic and pedestrians and particularly children before moving backwards. Keep a good look-out throughout.
2. Always turn your body and look over your shoulder in the direction the car is travelling. Never rely on the mirror. Hold one hand high and the other low on the wheel, or on the seat back to steady you.
3. Always reverse slowly to give maximum control of the car.
4. Never try to reverse the car when it is very close to the kerb, because the car will then run into the kerb whichever way the wheel is turned.
5. Turn the steering wheel to the left for a left-hand turn and to the right for a right-hand turn, just as in driving forward.
6. Keep the accelerator pedal in one position with the engine running gently, then vary the speed of the car by pressing or releasing the clutch. This enables you to move the car very slowly and gives time to correct errors in steering.
7. As you turn the wheel when moving backwards the front of the car moves sideways, so keep glancing to the front to ensure that the car is not getting too far off course. Because the front of your car swings out when you are reversing round the corner, it is important to keep a look-out for traffic approaching from your front and overtaking you as well as traffic in the opening to your rear. Be prepared to stop if necessary.

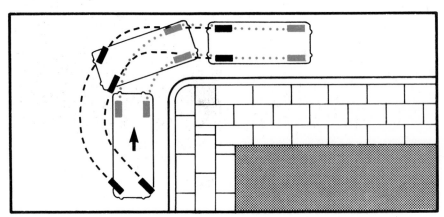

Diagram 32 Wheel tracks when reversing round a corner to the left

Reversing round a corner to the left

If the car is too close to the kerb, drive forward a few yards and position it about three or four feet from the kerb.

A Move the car slowly backwards, keeping parallel to the kerb (Photo 22).

B When the curve of the kerb appears in the corner of the rear quarter light (i.e., the rear of the car is approximately at the corner) turn the steering wheel quickly to the left (Photo 23). Because the front of the car will now swing out, check that all is still safe to your right (Photos 24 and 25).

C When the kerb disappears from the side window and reappears in the rear window, straighten the steering and check again for safety to the front (Photo 26).

D Continue reversing slowly and correct the steering until the car is straight (Photo 27).

Photo 22 A (see text)

Photo 23 B (see text)

Photo 24 Because the front of the car will now swing out . . .

Photo 25 . . .check that it is still safe to your right

Photo 26 C (see text)

Photo 27 D (see text)

Common faults

- Starting from a position too close to the kerb
- Turning too late and too slowly
- Straightening up too late and too slowly
- Not turning the wheel far enough
- Turning the steering wheel back too far after turning the corner
- Failing to keep a safe look-out for other road users

Reversing round a corner to the right

When reversing round a corner to the right, similar principles apply. However, the manoeuvre is simpler because the kerb edge can be seen out of the driver's window and the car steered accordingly.

Turning in the road using forward and reverse gears

This is sometimes called the '3-point turn' (though 5-point or even 7-point turns are quite allowable). It is useful where there are no openings or side turnings in which to turn round. It demonstrates mastery of the car's major controls as well as careful observation. Always move the car forwards from the left hand side of the road across to the right, and so on until the car is facing the opposite direction. This requires mastery of steering, forward and in reverse, selection of gears, good clutch control and careful use of clutch and hand brake together. The camber of the

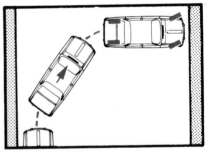

Diagram 33

1. Stop and engage the lowest gear

2. Look all round to ensure the road is clear. Move the car slowly forwards while turning the steering wheel to the right as quickly as possible

3. Reverse steering lock, press clutch and foot brake to stop the car before the front wheels touch the right-hand kerb

4. Apply hand brake and change into reverse gear

34

road sometimes makes this into a series of small 'hill starts'. Choose a place with good visibility and look round carefully for safety.

Never use the kerb as a buffer and be careful if you let your car overhang the kerb. It could cause danger to pedestrians or hit trees or lamp posts.

Always use the lowest gear and keep the clutch just slipping so that the car moves very slowly while you quickly turn the steering wheel from one 'lock' to the other.

Note

At 2, 6 and 10 use the clutch, accelerator and hand brake to do a 'hill start' (see page 23).

At the end of each move, forwards or backwards, when about three feet from the kerb turn the steering wheel quickly onto the opposite lock. This needs practice, but done properly lessens the time taken over the whole manoeuvre.

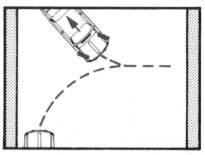

Diagram 34

5. Look all round to ensure the road is clear

6. Move the car slowly backwards, turning the wheel quickly further to the left if not already on full left lock

7. Before reaching kerb reverse lock to the right. Then press clutch and foot brake

8. Apply hand brake and change into first gear

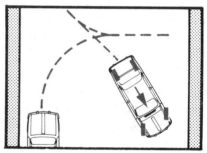

Diagram 35

9. Look all round to ensure the road is clear

10. Move the car forwards, with the steering wheel turned to the right until you either complete the turn and move away on the correct side of the road, or stop and reverse again following the same procedure

Pedestrian crossings

Zebra crossings

'Zebra' crossings are indicated by flashing yellow beacons and markings on the road. As soon as you see the zig-zag approach markings:
1. Keep a look-out for pedestrians on or near the crossing, and if there are pedestrians who look as though they may start to cross . . .
2. look in the mirror and slow down (signalling if necessary).

Do this in good time because you must always approach a pedestrian crossing at such a speed that you can stop if a pedestrian steps onto the crossing.

If pedestrians are actually *on* the crossing they have right of way and you are bound by law to stop at the 'give way' line. If there are pedestrians standing on the pavement waiting to cross, consider whether they are likely to have difficulty. You are not obliged to stop, but it may be helpful and is courteous to do so.

Except in an emergency, do not stop abruptly — always signal your intentions by arm (see signals, page 24). Before re-starting, look at both pavements and make sure that no one is on the crossing or about to step on to it.

It is an offence for drivers to wait or park on the zig-zag area, or on the approach side to overtake the leading vehicle which is moving, or which is stationary because it has stopped to let pedestrians cross.

Always be watchful and alert for the pedestrians who 'abuse' rather than use the crossings. Some people think that by putting a foot on the crossing everything will stop at once. Sometimes you will find it necessary to pull up really sharply because of such people. So be alert, look ahead for the flashing beacons and markings and make early and safe decisions.

Controlled crossings

Some pedestrian crossings may be controlled by push-buttons and lights (see page 16) or even though unmarked, by a policeman, traffic warden, or school crossing patrol, whose signals you must obey. At such crossings give way to pedestrians who are still crossing when the signal is given for vehicles to move on. If you are turning left or right at a junction, with traffic lights or not, give way to pedestrians who are crossing the side road. Beware of the pedestrian who does not wait for the lights to change and the traffic to stop. Because it happens to be your 'right of way' you are not entitled to run people down. The green traffic light is not a 'through' signal; it means that you may proceed *providing it is safe to do so.*

Photo 28 If pedestrians are actually on the crossing they have the right of way and you are bound by law to stop. If there are pedestrians standing on the pavement waiting to cross you are not obliged to stop, but it may be helpful and is courteous to do so

Photo 29 When slowing down or stopping for a pedestrian crossing you should signal by arm. This indicates to pedestrians as well as to following drivers that you are intending to stop

At zebras it is an offence to overtake the leading vehicle which has stopped to let pedestrians cross, or which is approaching the crossing and within the zig-zag lines. Such overtaking could endanger pedestrians

Crossroads

Major and light-controlled crossroads

Decide which course you are going to take well before the crossing, observing the road signs and markings so that you can approach in the correct lane, at a speed and in a gear which allows you to stop if the road is not clear; or if you are signalled to do so. Remember the junction procedure — 'MSM' and 'PSL'; use the mirror and signal well in advance of any turn or change of lane, looking right, left and right again when you reach a point from which you can see. Keep looking as you manoeuvre.

When turning to the left watch out for cyclists or motorcyclists on your left. Approach in the left-hand lane, giving way to pedestrians crossing the side road (car A in Diag. 36).

When going straight on you should normally use the left-hand lane unless it is obstructed ahead, or either the left or centre lane if there are three lanes in each direction. If there is a filter-left traffic signal do not use the left lane for going straight ahead. Beware of approaching traffic turning right, which should wait and pass behind you.

When turning right use the right-hand lane. Turn behind any approaching traffic and give way to pedestrians crossing the side road. Unless the crossroad is staggered, or road signs indicate otherwise, traffic turning right from opposite directions should pass right-hand to right-hand around the centre of the crossing (cars B and C in Diag. 36 and see page 31). Signal a right turn, move forward and wait at the turning point when permitted, allowing oncoming traffic to pass on your right-hand side. When the road is clear or the lights change to hold up oncoming traffic (Diag. 37), complete your turn to the right.

Quiet crossroads

The crossroads already mentioned are those on main or major roads. Once you are off these roads and in quiet residential or country areas it is possible to find many crossroads or intersections which do not have warning signs or road markings.

Many drivers think that because these roads are small, quiet and not signposted, no precautions are necessary. These minor junctions may be as dangerous as major ones and they must not be ignored. Slow down, change down and look out for other vehicles — look right, left and right again before proceeding.

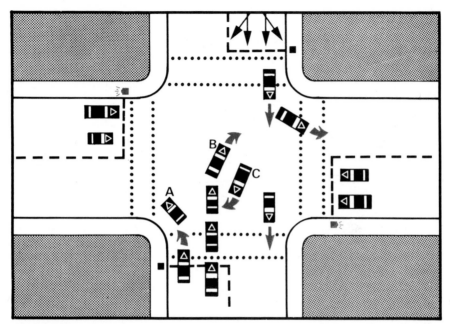

Diagram 36

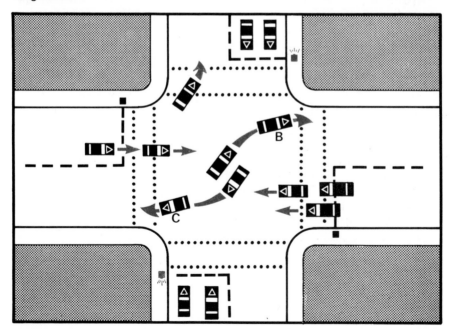

Diagram 37 Light-controlled crossroads

39

Entering major road from side road

When entering a major road from a side road, having used your mirror and given a signal, consider Position — Speed — Look. Your *Position* depends on whether turning left or right, leaving space if possible for following cars taking a different course, and how far forward it is safe and road markings permit you to move.

Speed must be slow enough to make a decision to continue or to stop, in the correct gear, without endangering others and while obeying road signs and markings.

Look means knowing the situation on the main road, and beside and behind you. Be particularly careful to notice approaching motorcycles. Look right, left, right again, but continue looking as you move out.

Turning right into busy major road

Use mirror, signal with right indicator and position car just left of the side-road centre (Diag. 39). Move forward to Stop or Give Way road markings, or (if there are none) to a point where you can see in both directions without impeding main road traffic.

First watch traffic from the right, looking well back; then, when the right is clear, look left for a break in the traffic there. When you see a gap to the left, look right again and if it is still clear there move slowly forward, ready to accelerate and join in behind the last car or cars preceding the gap ('A' and 'B' in Diag. 39). Drive on only when you are sure it is safe to do so.

Never turn abruptly across the path of approaching vehicles (from either direction), and never cut a right-hand corner, otherwise there will be insufficient room for vehicles entering the road you are leaving.

When turning right out of a narrow side road, wide enough for only one line of traffic in each direction, or little more, keep well to the left of the side road before emerging, to leave space for other vehicles entering. Ensure you know approaching cars' intentions before you pull out (Diag. 40).

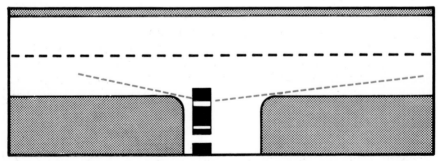

Diagram 38 Look both ways along the major road

40

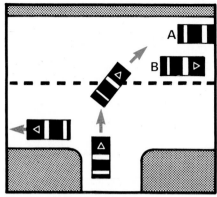

Diagram 39 Turning right into a busy main road

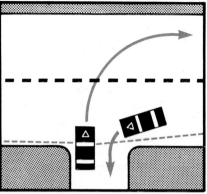

Diagram 40 Turning right from a narrow side road

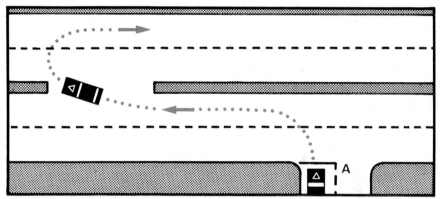

Diagram 41 Turning right into a dual carriageway with no break directly opposite in the centre island

Turning right into dual carriageway

You will often find that the centre island has no break in it directly opposite the side road (see Diag. 41).

Slow down and stop at the line A. MSM — PSL is vital.

When traffic from the right allows, turn left and then use your right-hand direction indicator. Move towards the central reservation and look for a gap through it. Turn into this gap. If you stop, make sure you are clear of traffic on both carriageways and look for traffic from the left. When this traffic allows, complete your turn to the right and gradually pull over to the nearside lane.

Turning left

Turning left at any of these roads is much easier. Stop in the left-hand lane and wait until the traffic from the right is clear, then turn into the main road.

Roundabouts

The roundabout, including the mini-roundabout, is simply an inter-section of roads where traffic streams mix, with an island in the centre. All traffic on the roundabout must travel in a clockwise direction. Good all-round observation is necessary, speed must be reduced and a lower gear engaged before entering.

Traffic approaching a roundabout must give way to vehicles already on it, points of entry being marked by broken white lines on the road. In exceptional cases priority may be given to traffic *entering* the round-about, and this would be indicated by 'Give way' markings across the carriageway in the roundabout (see page 14).

On the approach, use your mirror to see what is following or what is about to overtake you, consider if a signal is necessary, reduce speed, change gear and filter into your correct approach lane. Look out for pedestrians crossing (some roundabouts have pedestrian crossings near the entry or exit points). If clear, proceed into the roundabout, giving way to traffic coming from the right and staying in your chosen lane through the roundabout.

If, to get to the exit you want, you have to pass one or more of the other entries into the roundabout then you must watch for traffic enter-ing from these roads on your left, although this traffic should give way to you.

There may be several things to do while driving round a roundabout. You must watch other drivers' signals as the traffic streams mix. Be prepared for others to cross your path, and watch long vehicles particu-larly — they may steer a different course.

You must be alert and observant. Be prepared for traffic to overtake you on your right- and/or left-hand side and use your mirror or mirrors to know that they are about to pass you. Remember MSM. Do not be afraid of stopping or giving way; try to maintain the traffic flow but do not rush or be aggressive.

To turn left, approach by the left-hand lane, stay in this lane and leave by it, keeping your left-hand indicator working throughout (Diag. 42).

To go in a forward direction, drive in the left or right-hand lane, as indicated by circumstances, and give a left signal as you pass the exit before the one by which you wish to leave. Leave in the left-hand lane unless conditions dictate using the right-hand lane (Diags. 42 and 43).

To turn right, keep in the right-hand lane, using your right indicator on approach and throughout the roundabout, until switching to a left signal on passing the exit before the one by which you wish to leave. Then leave as above (Diag. 43).

Diags. 42 – 45 show the principles to observe, for normal and for mini-roundabouts. Apply them with common sense, and if you are sure there is no other traffic it is permissible to steer through the roundabout by the most direct route.

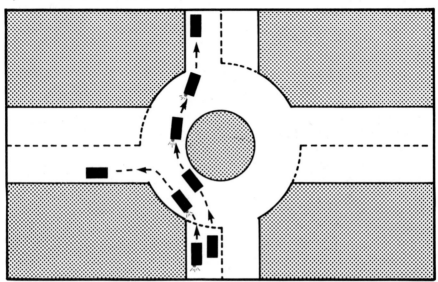

Diagram 42

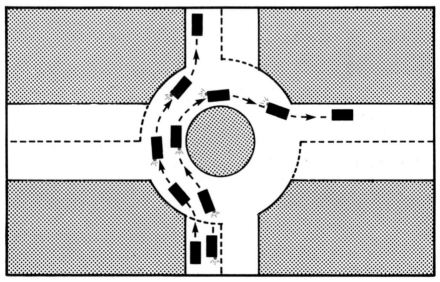

Diagram 43 Basic routes and signalling

NOTE: Each entry road is marked with a transverse broken white line indicating 'give way'

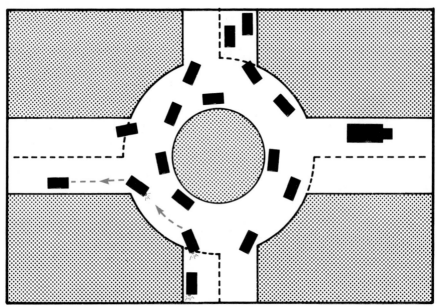

Diagram 44 Turning left

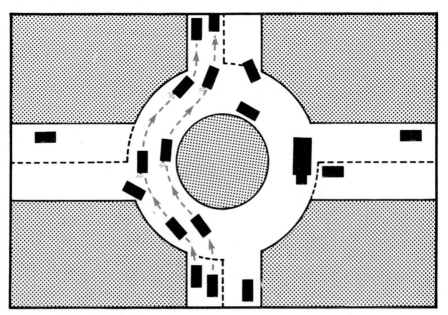

Diagram 45 Straight ahead

More examples with traffic; for simplicity only the car in question is showing signalling

44

Overtaking and stopping
Overtaking

Note what the Highway Code says on this subject. Pulling out into the approaching traffic's lane, either to pass a stationary object or to overtake a moving vehicle, needs careful judgement of the different speeds of yourself and of all other vehicles, and of the distances needed and available. The rate of overtaking is only the difference between your speed and the speed of the vehicle you are overtaking, but the rate of approach of an oncoming vehicle is the sum of its speed and yours. So the distance you need clear before starting to overtake is the distance an approaching car can cover — plus a safety margin — in the time you need to pull out, accelerate, pass and return to your side of the road without cutting in.

Before overtaking make sure that the road is clear ahead and behind, that you have the acceleration if required, and that it is safe for yourself and others to overtake. *If in doubt hold back*. Remember Mirror — Signal — Manoeuvre. Overtake on the right except ·as stated in the Highway Code.

There are certain occasions when you should never overtake. Learn these carefully from the Highway Code.

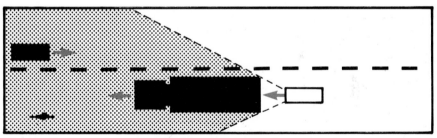

Diagram 46 Car too close to lorry. Car driver cannot see cyclist or car coming the other way. If he pulls out, he risks a head-on collision

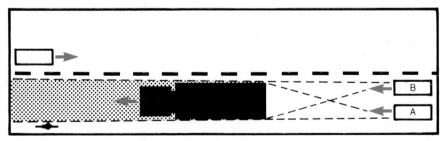

Diagram 47 Car correct distance from lorry. In position A the car driver can see obstructions a short distance in front of the lorry and by moving out only a little (position B) he can see oncoming traffic. He also has more distance in which to accelerate so that the actual overtaking time is reduced

Be particularly careful on three-lane roads, and at dusk, or in fog or mist, when it is difficult to judge speed and distance. Never follow a leading overtaking vehicle through without first checking for yourself. What is safe for another may not be safe for you.

The procedure for overtaking moving vehicles is:

1. position yourself safely where you can see ahead. Engage the right gear giving adequate speed and acceleration, and assess the situation ahead. If safe ahead,
2. look in the mirror to make sure that a vehicle is not about to overtake you,
3. signal with right-hand indicator,
4. check ahead and behind again, and overtake quickly, not passing too close but pulling out and returning in a smooth curve. Check in your mirror that you are not cutting in.

Overtaking on hills requires a longer distance. Going uphill reduces acceleration, while going downhill increases the braking distance should you need to slow down at an obstruction or stop. When descending a hill with an obstruction, either on the left or right, give way to approaching vehicles which are climbing.

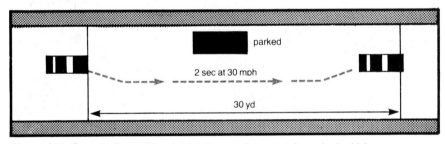

Diagram 48 Car travelling at 30 mph takes 2 seconds to overtake parked vehicle

Double white lines
A double white line along the middle of the road means:

If the line nearer to you is continuous, keep to your own side of it and do not cross or straddle it.

If the line nearer to you is broken you may cross it to overtake, but only if you can see that it is safe to do so and that you can complete your overtaking before reaching a continuous white line on your side.

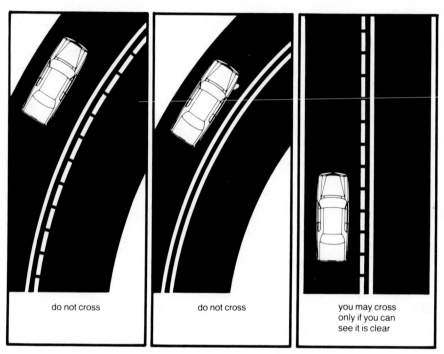

Diagram 49 Double white lines

Stopping

The *stopping distance* for a car is made up of two parts — your *thinking distance* plus the *braking distance*. These can vary enormously, depending on your skill and alertness as a driver, your speed, the conditions of your brakes and tyres, the weather and state of the road and whether you are going up or down a hill.

As a driver you should know the overall stopping distance needed for the speed at which you are travelling. In good conditions this may be as shown in the table.

Stopping distance at various speeds in good conditions

mph	Thinking distance ft	+	Braking distance ft	=	Overall stopping distance ft
30	30		45 $(1\frac{1}{2} \times)$		75
40	40		80 $(2 \times)$		120
50	50		125 $(2\frac{1}{2} \times)$		175
60	60		180 $(3 \times)$		240
70	70		245 $(3\frac{1}{2} \times)$		315

The absolute safe rule is to leave this overall stopping distance from the car in front, increasing the gap much more in wet or icy conditions. But on the open road in good conditions a rough guide, which at over 40 mph gives less than the overall stopping distance, is to leave one yard per mph of your speed. This is equivalent to 2 seconds travelling time, hence the '2 second rule'. You should be able to count 'one second, two seconds' as the preceding car passes a point and before you do so too.

When following another vehicle remember:

1. Allow more than one yard per mph if conditions are not good, or whenever possible as speed rises above 40 mph.
2. If closer than your overall stopping distance you may be taking some risk.
3. If closer than your thinking distance you are driving in considerable danger.
4. If a vehicle reduces your gap by overtaking, lengthen the space again by dropping back.

Night and difficult conditions

When driving at night, make sure your windscreen is clean inside and out, your lights correctly adjusted and in working order. Remember, by day or night regardless of the conditions you must be able to stop within the distance you can see to be clear. Look carefully for cycles and motorcycles, which present only a small profile. Cycles are frequently badly lit.

In a built-up area at night you should drive more slowly than in daylight and take great care where there are patches of light and shadow, as pedestrians are often difficult to see under these conditions. Until dim-dipped headlights are an obligatory fitting (on new cars from 1987), if the street lighting is not good switch on your headlights and drive with them dipped. You must use normal headlamps on all roads where there is no street lighting.

If you are dazzled by approaching headlights, keep well to the left, slow down and even stop if necessary. Look at the left-hand kerb to keep your eyes from the glare. Always dip your headlights when other traffic is approaching and also when following behind other vehicles, before you are close enough for your lights to dazzle other drivers.

If you are troubled by glare in your driving mirror, move your head or body so that you become out of range of the reflected lights. A dipping mirror is useful.

Park with side lights (*not* headlights) at night, close to the kerb and (except in one-way streets) only on the left. In a 30 mph (or less) limit you may park as above without lights, but not within 15 yards of a junction.

In rain, snow, fog or on icy roads reduce speed according to the severity of the conditions. Do not park where you are likely to cause an obstruction. During daylight you must use headlights — or side-lights and foglights — when visibility is seriously reduced, to see and be seen. Use rear fog lights too, but switch them off when they are no longer essential. In rain or snow, or on icy roads, cut the risk of skidding by avoiding sudden movements of any kind — braking, accelerating or steering.

If the car skids on a slippery road, do not panic and do not immediately press the foot brake. Take your foot off the accelerator, leave the brakes and try to get the four wheels in line with the road again by turning the steering wheel in the *same* direction as the skid. Beware of over-steering, which can cause a skid in the other direction. If it is necessary to use the brakes then they should be used gently with a pumping action of on–off–on.

When you think of skidding you usually think of icy, snowy or wet roads, but remember that dry surfaces with loose grit, sand or gravel are also very dangerous, as are slightly damp roads after a dry spell.

Most important of all, a good driver does not skid: he avoids skidding by anticipation and correct precautions. Too high a speed, leading to excessive braking, cornering or steering is the commonest cause of skidding, and speed must be reduced where the road surface is at all loose or slippery. It is easier to get into a skid than out of it. Anticipate, and accelerate, brake and steer gently.

Parking in a limited space

Parking between two cars at the kerb-side is a manoeuvre which has to be done frequently in towns, and it needs much practice before you can do it well. It is sensible to reduce any risk to other cars by making your first attempts in reasonably quiet roads, with bricks or chalk marks indicating the two parked cars.

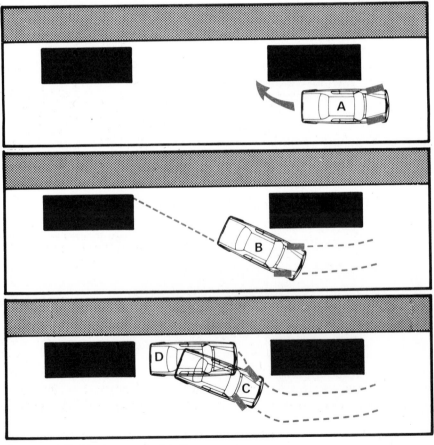

Diagram 50 Parking by reversing into the space

50

Always reverse into the space. An adequate space is 1½ car lengths. It is a good plan to start practising with more space than this, and to reduce it as the exercise becomes easier. Going far enough forward is important. Remember MSM when manoeuvring.

The method is shown in Diag. 50. The reason for reversing into the space is that you can move the front of the car sideways but not the back. Therefore, if the rear end is put into the space first, the front can be made to follow.

When parked, leave enough room for other cars to get away; do not, however, be wasteful of kerb-side space, which may be needed by another driver.

Photo 30 Drive well forward, stopping half-a-length past, parallel to and one-and-a-half to three feet out from the next parked car

Photo 31 Check traffic behind and in front. If safe, reverse slowly (A in Diag. 50), turning the steering wheel to the left (Photo 32) until . . .

Photo 32

Photo 33 the kerbside headlight of the parked car at the rear appears in the offside of your rear window (B in Diag. 50)

Photo 34 Straighten the front wheels and move slowly backwards until the left front of your car just clears the rear corner of the parked car in front (C in Diag. 50)

Photo 35 Now turn the steering wheel quickly full lock to the right

Photo 36 . . . and continue slowly backwards

Photo 37 Straighten up as the car runs parallel with the kerb (D in Diag. 50), and if necessary move the car forward a short distance to give equal space back and front

Part 3: Taking the test
Hints on taking your test
Read carefully, re-read and comply with the instructions in the official leaflet, *Your driving test and how to pass*, issued with your provisional licence and frequently called the DL 68. Make sure your car is in a thoroughly sound, roadworthy condition.

Throughout your training have adequate professional instruction and practice, making sure you know exactly what the driving test comprises. See page 64 for information about RAC Registered instructors. Before going to take your test, check your appointment card and be sure that you have the correct date, time and place.

Practically everybody taking the test is nervous. This is quite natural, but once you have met the examiner and listened to his instructions, you should concentrate entirely on your driving, bearing in mind the correct control and road procedures listed in the DL 68. In this way you will help yourself to overcome any nervous tension.

Drive normally and naturally, remembering the things you have been taught, but do not put on a special 'show'.

Do not look for catches, or trick questions, because the test is carried out in a fair and straightforward manner. You will not be asked to do anything you have not been taught; that is, of course, if you have had good professional tuition and have followed the syllabus in the DL 68. The examiner is trained to give brief, standardised instructions in order to avoid any possibility of confusion or of distracting you from your driving.

If during the test you make a mistake, rectify it if possible and then continue with the test. Do not give up, thinking that because you have made one mistake you have failed. Most examinees make one or more mistakes during the test, and provided that they are not dangerous or of major importance, and that the same mistakes do not recur — then it is still possible to drive to the required standard. The examiner is looking for a driver who is basically safe and who will acquire more expertise with practice.

The Highway Code
Questions
Here is a selection of typical questions which you may be asked on the Code. The answers are on page 56.

1. For whom is the Highway Code written?
2. To what fourteen points should you pay particular attention when keeping your car in good condition?
3. When should you not use the horn?
4. What must you do when driving in the dark?
5. When should you not increase your speed?
6. When should you never overtake?
7. How should you overtake under normal conditions?
8. When can you pass other traffic on the nearside (left-hand side)?
9. Where should you not park?
10. When should you give signals?
11. When should you use the mirror?
12. At what speed should you approach pedestrian crossings or traffic lights?
13. What do you know about pedestrian crossings?
14. Before driving a car what must you be sure about?
15. Many road signs have a triangle or a circle. Why should some have one and some the other?
16. What sign could you expect to see at the entrance of a minor road into a major road?
17. What is the procedure when you approach a sign which says 'STOP'?
18. What is the procedure when you are approaching a sign which says 'GIVE WAY'?
19. What must you do if involved in an accident?
20. Who has the authority to stop and start traffic on the road?
21. When passing a long line of parked cars, what would you be looking for?
22. When is it possible to drive on against the red traffic lights?
23. Do you know the sequence of changes of the traffic lights?
24. What causes skidding?
25. When is a driver considered to be in an unfit condition to drive?
26. What must always be kept clean on a car?
27. At what distance should you drive behind the preceding vehicle?
28. What should you do when you see a double white line along the middle of the road?
29. When using mechanical indicators, what must you always be sure about?
30. If, when attempting to overtake, you find that the other vehicle

begins to accelerate, what action should you take?
31. Where should you not reverse?
32. How should you reverse?
33. When stopping at the side of the road, what is the correct procedure?

Motorway driving

34. There are four things that you often find on normal main roads that are not found on motorways. What are they?
35. When using the motorways, what six things are of utmost importance?
36. Who and what are not allowed on the motorways?
37. How should you counter drowsiness while driving on the motorway?
38. How do you enter a motorway?
39. If you miss the exit from the motorway that you intend to take, what must you do?
40. Under the same circumstances as in question 39, what must you not do?
41. If your car breaks down or is involved in an accident, what must you do to it?
42. What do you know about motorway lane discipline?

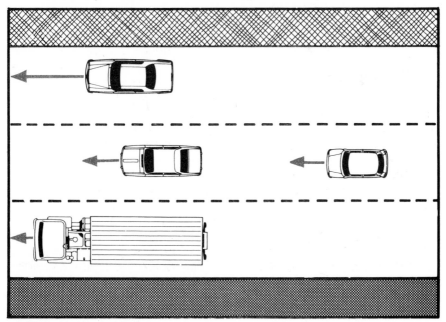

Diagram 51 (See question 42)

Answers to Highway Code questions

1. For all road users, pedestrians, motorists, cyclists, etc.
2. Lights, brakes, steering, tyres, demisters, windscreen wipers and washers. Keep windscreens, windows, lights, direction indicators, reflectors, mirrors and number plates clean and clear.
3. In a built-up area between the hours of 11-30 p.m. and 7-0 a.m. and when the car is stationary (except in times of danger due to another moving vehicle).
4. Make sure all lamps work and headlamps are properly adjusted. If dazzled slow down or stop. Drive so that you can stop well within the distance you can see to be clear. Use headlights where there is no street lighting, and dipped headlights in built-up areas, unless the street lighting is so good that they are not needed. Dip headlamps when meeting other road users and before they dazzle the drivers of vehicles travelling in front in the same direction.
5. When being overtaken.
6. Never overtake unless you are sure that you can do so without danger to yourself and others. This includes such circumstances as when approaching a pedestrian crossing, road junction, at corners or bends, a brow of a hill, hump-back bridge or level crossing; where the road narrows; where the road is marked with double white lines and the nearest to you is continuous if this would involve crossing the continuous line; where to overtake would force other traffic to swerve or reduce speed; after a No Overtaking sign.
7. Only on the right. Use Mirror — Signal — Manoeuvre and check that it is safe in front and behind; once you have started, overtake quickly, leaving plenty of room. Move back to the left without cutting in.
8. When the car in front is turning right and you can safely do so without impeding others; when you are turning left at a junction; when traffic is moving slowly in queues and vehicles on the right are moving more slowly than you are; in one-way streets (but not dual carriageways) where vehicles can pass on either side.
9. A car should not be parked or left standing where you see a no waiting or a clearway sign, yellow lines beside the kerb (except at permitted times), or double white lines in the middle of the road; where it would make it difficult for others to see clearly, i.e., at or near a junction, bend, brow of a hill, hump-back bridge or level crossing; where it would be a danger to other road users, i.e. at or near a bus stop, on or either side of a pedestrian crossing, at or near a school entrance, on a footpath, pavement or cycle path, on the right-hand side of the road at night (except in a one-way street), or where it would hide a traffic sign; where it would hold up traffic or

inconvenience others, i.e., on a narrow road, on flyovers, in tunnels or in underpasses (unless there are signs to say you may park there), on fast main roads (except in a lay-by), on motorways (except on the hard shoulder in an emergency), on a single track road, or in a passing place on such a road, outside a private entrance for vehicles, where emergency vehicles stop or go in and out, hospital entrances, doctors' entrances, fire stations, fire hydrants, where you would make the road narrow, opposite an island, alongside another parked vehicle, opposite another parked vehicle if this would narrow the road to less than the width of two vehicles, near road works. Always park your vehicle safely. Walk a few more yards rather than cause an accident.

10. In good time and if they would help or warn other road users.
11. Often; and always before you move off from rest, open the car door, signal, change course, overtake, turn, slow or stop.
12. At a speed at which you can stop if necessary.
13. There are two types of pedestrian crossing. The zebra crossing, where pedestrians have right of way; and controlled crossings, where pedestrians should proceed only in conjunction with the traffic lights or policeman, according to how the traffic is being controlled. 'Pelicans' are increasingly common.
14. That the vehicle is properly licensed and has a current MOT test certificate; that you are complying with the law regarding insurance; that you have a valid and signed driving licence for the type of vehicle you are going to drive; and that you are not under the influence of drink or drugs. Last and not least, that the vehicle is in a roadworthy condition as required by law.
15. Signs with a triangle, base down, are warning and informative: they give no instructions, only information that certain hazards are ahead. All signs with a circle are mandatory, and so is the GIVE WAY sign in an inverted triangle; that is, you must obey these signs or you will be breaking the law. The blue circle signs tell you what to do and the red circle signs are prohibitive or restrictive. See page 15.
16. Either STOP (red octagonal) or GIVE WAY (in an inverted triangle).
17. Stop in the correct lane at the transverse stop line at the major road, and do not proceed until you can do so without causing danger or inconvenience to any vehicle on the major road.
18. Approach the major road with due caution in the correct lane, and do not cross the transverse double broken lines, unless this can be done without causing danger or inconvenience to any vehicle on the major road.
19. Stop, give driver's and vehicle owner's names and addresses, with

vehicle registration number. If there is any personal injury you are also obliged to show your certificate of insurance at the time, to a police officer or other person having reasonable grounds to see it. If the above is not done for any reason report to the police as soon as practicable and within 24 hours.

20. A police officer in uniform, a traffic warden on traffic control duty, a school crossing patrol in uniform displaying a 'Stop — children' sign to enable children to cross the road on their way to and from school.

21. Pedestrians walking or running from between cars, offside doors opening, and cars pulling out from the kerb without signs or signals. Be specially careful if these cars are parked outside schools. Watch for children.

22. When there is a green filter arrow attached to the lights. It is possible to proceed when the arrow lights up, but only in the direction of the arrow.

23. Red to red and amber, then green, then amber only, then red.

24. Sharp, hard braking, sharp acceleration, sharp movements of the steering and excessive speed on icy, wet, leafy or loose-surface roads.

25. When he is under the influence of alcohol or drugs, or is fatigued.

26. The windscreen and all windows and mirrors used for observation by the driver, also the number plates, direction indicators, reflectors and lights.

27. The distance you need to react and stop if traffic in front stops suddenly. This depends on your speed, your alertness, the condition of your brakes, tyres, the weather and the road. You should always be at a distance within which you can stop if the traffic in front comes to a sudden halt.

28. If the line nearer you is continuous, keep to your own side of it and do not cross or straddle it. If the line nearer to you is broken you may cross it, but only if you can see that it is safe to do so and that you can complete overtaking before reaching a continuous white line on your side.

29. (a) That they convey the message intended and (b) that they are cancelled immediately after use.

30. Slow down and drop back into line.

31. Into a main road.

32. With great care; make sure that there are no children or pedestrians or obstructions behind you and that you can see all round. If in doubt get help.

33. Use the mirror, give the appropriate signal, draw in gently and pull in as close as possible to the kerb.

Motorway driving

34. Sharp bends, junctions on the right, roundabouts and traffic lights.
35. Quicker reading of traffic situations, use of the mirror, concentration, that your car is fit to cruise at speed, that it has correct tyre pressures, and that it has enough petrol, oil and water to reach the next service area.
36. Pedestrians, learner drivers, pedal cycles, motorcycles with engines of 50 cc or below, invalid carriages, agricultural vehicles, animals and heavy vehicles carrying over-size loads (except with special permission).
37. Keep the car well ventilated, and periodically stop at parking or service areas and stretch your legs. A cup of coffee, if available, may also help.
38. From an access point at the end of a slip road, watch for a gap in the nearside and give way to traffic already on the motorway. Accelerate in the extra (acceleration) lane and join the nearside lane travelling at the same speed as the traffic already on it.
39. Continue until you reach the next exit.
40. Reverse or turn in the carriageway, drive against the traffic or cross the central reservation.
41. Get the car off the carriageway and onto the verge. You must not walk on the carriageway.
42. After joining the motorway stay in the nearside lane until you are used to the speed. On a two-lane carriageway drive in the left-hand lane except when overtaking. On a three-lane carriageway stay in the middle lane when slower vehicles fill the inside lane, but return to the nearside lane when you have passed them. The outer lane is for overtaking only; if you use it move back into the middle lane (without cutting in) and then into the inside lane as soon as you can.

Do's and don'ts
Do
1. DO make sure your vehicle is ready for the road before you start up and drive off.
2. DO make sure your driving licence is in order, up-to-date and allows you to drive the particular type or class of vehicle. Also make sure that you are complying with the law regarding insurance. This *must* be properly checked, especially if the car has been loaned to you.
3. DO adjust your seat so that you are comfortable and can reach the pedals without stretching. Adjust the mirror or mirrors and be sure that the windscreen and windows are clean so that your observation is in no way impaired.
4. DO wear your seat belt. It is compulsory (as from January 1983) for drivers and front-seat passengers of cars and other vehicles fitted with seat belts to wear them. There are a few exemptions, including drivers when reversing.
5. DO make sure that your gear lever is in the neutral position before starting the engine.
6. DO use your mirror and glance over your right shoulder to make sure that it is safe before moving away from the kerb.
7. DO look well ahead while driving and drive at a speed at which you can stop in the distance you can see to be clear. Except in an emergency, avoid sharp, hard braking and sharp movements with the steering; in this way it should be possible to avoid skidding.
8. DO be patient with other road users. Impatient drivers cause accidents. Drive defensively, to foresee possible danger and to avoid it.
9. DO use your mirror constantly and appreciate what you see in it.
10. DO give special attention and care to children, the aged and infirm.
11. DO stop if you have an accident, or if you are requested to do so by a policeman.
12. DO read and understand the Highway Code and keep up-to-date with all the rules and regulations.
13. DO ensure that your car is always in a thoroughly roadworthy condition and has good brakes, good tyres (at correct pressures), lights and steering.

Don't

1. DO NOT drive if you are mentally or physically unable to control your vehicle, through fatigue, drink, drugs, or some physical ailment that is perhaps temporary. Present-day traffic conditions call for 100% efficiency from all road users.
2. DO NOT disregard road signs or signals. Read the road as you would read a book. There are full stops and commas, halts, pauses and queries. Read it all and understand what you are reading.
3. DO NOT think that you are the perfect driver, immune from faults and accidents. Always be on the alert and ready for any emergency.
4. DO NOT show off in front of other people. This will make you reckless, careless and prone to mistakes and accidents.
5. DO NOT attempt to race other cars on public roads.
6. DO NOT drive in the centre of the road when it is possible to drive on the left. Road 'hogging' is dangerous.
7. DO NOT alter course or speed without first consulting your mirror, making sure that it is safe to do so and signalling in good time when necessary.
8. DO NOT drive anywhere, or at any time, at a speed at which you feel uncomfortable or incapable of controlling your vehicle and fully reading the road. Know your own limits and drive within them.
9. DO NOT forget that there are many other road users. A little courtesy and respect for them cost nothing, and are signs not only of good driving but of good manners.
10. DO NOT expect the other fellow always to do the correct thing — he probably won't. Anticipate the unexpected and never presume that events will follow their correct or a particular course.

Accident prevention

Even when you have passed your test you have only proved that you know the basic principles of car driving and the Highway Code. There is still plenty to learn afterwards and only careful and considerate driving will keep you accident-free.

If you are involved in an accident . . .
1. Stop.
2. Take the number of any passing vehicle whose occupants may have seen the accident. Even if it did not stop, it can be traced through the licensing authorities.
3. Take names and addresses of any witnesses on the spot. If you have a camera, photograph the vehicles before they are moved, and any marks or debris on the road.
4. If there are no personal injuries, exchange names, addresses and details of drivers and vehicle ownership with the other people involved. There is no need to call the police. Make no apologies or admissions of liability.
5. If there are personal injuries, it is advisable to call the police, but not essential as long as the particulars are exchanged and drivers are able to produce their insurance certificates.
6. In either case, if particulars are not exchanged then the accident must be reported to the police as soon as possible and in any case within 24 hours.

RAC Register of Instructors
RAC Motoring Services Limited
P.O. Box 100, RAC House, Lansdowne Road, Croydon, CR9 2JA
Tel: 01-686 2525

With the advent of the compulsory driving test in 1935, the Royal Automobile Club instituted its voluntary and impartial system of testing and registration of driving instructors. Today, when all professional instructors must by law be Government-approved, the RAC Register continues, indicating that RAC Registered driving instructors are men and women of the highest calibre who quite voluntarily have obtained a further qualification to teach driving from a completely independent and impartial body.

Learning to drive with an RAC Registered instructor is therefore an extra guarantee that your instructor has the ability to teach, a complete knowledge of the subject and a high standard of integrity.

Names and addresses of RAC Registered instructors can be obtained from any RAC Office or from the address above.

Index